D0590936

SUNDAY LUNCH

— WITH —

Mrs BEETON

TRADITIONAL CLASSICS

SUNDAY LUNCH

— WITH —

Mrs BEETON

TRADITIONAL CLASSICS

WARD LOCK

First published 1990 by Ward Lock
Villiers House, 41/47 Strand, London WC2N 5JE, England

A Cassell imprint

© Text and illustrations Ward Lock Limited 1990

Designed by Cherry Randell
Illustrations by Mike Shoebridge
Edited by Alison Leach and Helen Douglas-Cooper

Typeset in Goudy Old Style by Litho Link Ltd, Welshpool, Powys, Wales

Printed and bound in Italy by Olivotto

British Library Cataloguing in Publication Data
Beeton, Mrs, 1836-1865
 Sunday lunch with Mrs. Beeton.
 1. Sunday luncheons – Recipes
 I. Title
 641.53

ISBN 0-7063-6890-8

CONTENTS

INTRODUCTION

During the first half of the nineteenth century the pattern of meal times for the wealthy began to change. The poor, working classes continued to breakfast, lunch and dine on whatever food they could get, but by the 1860s, meals for the increasingly wealthy middle and upper classes became larger and more elaborate. Breakfast, which had in previous centuries been taken at 9 or 10 in the morning was now eaten at 8, and was a hearty affair. Lunch remained a fairly light meal at about 1 o'clock. If a lady was alone she sometimes ate with her children, or had soup and a sandwich on her own. If she was entertaining, dishes would have been dainty rather than filling, but still the meal was not a large one.

Dinner until the first decade of the century had usually been served at 5 or 6 o'clock in the evening, but because of the demands of the work routine, the establishment of gentlemen's clubs which kept the men from their homes until well into the evening, and because of the amount of visiting done, dinner was now served at 8, 9, or 10 o'clock. In the eighteenth century,

fancy sandwiches, trifles, jellies, creams and cakes. In contrast a family supper would have been a simple affair of cold meats, stewed fruit, cheese and biscuits.

In all these eating activities the servants obviously played a major part – setting tables, folding napkins, polishing silver, arranging flowers, cooking the food, serving the food and attending at table. Their work started well before breakfast and ended when the last member of the family had retired for the night. But, on Sunday afternoons they were usually given a free half-day, so a full meal was cooked and served for the family at lunch time, and then the servants disappeared to enjoy their short time of freedom. Cook left ready a cold supper which the family could manage without help, and so the tradition of Sunday lunch began. Many families around Britain still sit down together at Sunday lunchtime to enjoy a roast meal and all the traditional trimmings.

a family dinner would have consisted of three or four savoury dishes and two desserts. A formal dinner, however, consisted of two complete meals, one set out after the other, from which guests selected a variety of sweet and savoury foods. This changed in Victorian times to a grand repast where dishes of the same type were served together – soups and fish, then roast meats and made-up dishes, then vegetables and sweets and finally dessert. There were up to seven courses, and even a modest dinner for six or seven people could involve thirteen or fourteen dishes plus desserts.

Supper dances and receptions were also popular and played a major part in Victorian nightlife. The food at these was generally a cold buffet of salmon mayonnaise, lobster patties, poultry, tongue,

$\mathcal{S}$TARTERS

Introduce Sunday lunch with a light starter that does not
leave guests too full to enjoy the vast array of delicious food
that follows. In winter choose warming soups. In summer
serve chilled, crisp vegetables or salads.

SPRING LUNCH

marinated melon

crown of lamb
mint sauce
potatoes Anna
spring peas
glazed carrots

lemon meringue pie
orange soufflé

MARINATED MELON

2 Ogen **or** Charentais melons
60 ml/4 tbsp maraschino liqueur
or port

Cut the melons in half crossways
and scoop out the seeds. Spoon
15 ml/1 tbsp of maraschino liqueur
or port into the centre and chill for
1 hour before serving. Sugar can be
served with the melons as well, if
desired.

SERVES 4

ASPARAGUS WITH HOT LEMON SAUCE

50 heads asparagus
250 ml/8 fl oz milk
1 small lettuce, finely shredded
1 small onion, chopped
1 bay leaf
1 sprig of thyme
salt
25 g/1 oz butter
25 g/1 oz flour
1 egg
pepper
5 ml/1 tsp lemon juice
8 slices toasted **or** *fried bread*

Garnish
chopped parsley
cucumber strips

Prepare the asparagus heads and tie them into bundles. Put the milk into a deep saucepan or asparagus pan. Add the lettuce and onion to the pan with the bay leaf, thyme, and a little salt. Bring the milk to the boil and put in the asparagus. Simmer gently for about 15 minutes or until the asparagus is tender.

Remove from the pan and trim off all the inedible parts of the stalks. Untie, and keep the asparagus warm. Strain the milk.

Melt the butter in a small clean saucepan, stir in the flour, and cook gently for 1 minute. Draw off the heat and gradually stir in the strained milk. Return to the heat and stir all the time until the sauce thickens. Cool slightly, beat the egg until liquid, and stir it into the sauce. Season to taste, and add the lemon juice.

Arrange the slices of toast or fried bread on a warmed serving dish, and pile the asparagus on them. Coat with the sauce and garnish with chopped parsley and cucumber strips.

SERVES 4

AVOCADOS WITH PRAWNS OR AVOCADO ROYALE

30 ml/2 tbsp olive oil
30 ml/2 tbsp distilled vinegar
a pinch each of salt and pepper
a little mixed French mustard (not Dijon)
2 large avocados
a pinch of sugar (optional)
½ garlic clove (optional), crushed
100 g/4 oz peeled prawns, fresh, frozen or canned
crisp lettuce leaves
lemon wedges to garnish

Blend the oil, vinegar and seasonings together.

Halve and stone the pears, and brush all over with a little of the dressing. Add the sugar and garlic to the remaining dressing, if used. Toss the prawns in this; then spoon into the avocado halves.

Place on crisp lettuce leaves. Garnish with lemon wedges.

Note Frozen prawns should be squeezed gently before using to get rid of excess moisture.

SERVES 4

JERUSALEM ARTICHOKE SOUP

500 g/18 oz Jerusalem artichokes
white vinegar
25 g/1 oz butter **or** *margarine*
1 onion, chopped
500 ml/17 fl oz white stock
lemon juice
salt and pepper
125 ml/4½ fl oz milk
20 ml/4 tsp cornflour for each 500 ml/
17 fl oz puréed soup
cold stock, water **or** *milk*
60 ml/4 tbsp single cream (optional)

Scrape the artichokes and put each one into water acidulated with a little vinegar. Rinse and dry them with absorbent kitchen paper.

Melt the fat in a deep saucepan, add the vegetables, and fry gently for 5–10 minutes without browning them. Add the stock, lemon juice, and seasoning to taste. Heat to boiling point, reduce the heat, and simmer gently until the vegetables are quite soft. Do not overcook.

Purée the vegetables and liquid by either pushing through a fine sieve, or by processing in a blender. Add the milk, measure the soup, and return it to a clean pan. Measure the cornflour in the correct proportion and blend it with a little cold stock, water or milk. Stir it into the soup. Bring to the boil, stirring all the time, and cook for 5 minutes. Adjust seasoning if required.

Serve with croûtons, Melba or fairy toast.

To make a Cream of Jerusalem Artichoke Soup, remove the pan from the heat after the soup has been thickened and leave to cool slightly. Add a little of the hot soup to the single cream (which can replace some of the milk in the main recipe) and beat well. Whisk the mixture into the rest of the soup. Return the soup to gentle heat and reheat, without boiling, stirring all the time.

SERVES 4

JELLIED TOMATO SOUP WITH SOURED CREAM

*400 g/14 oz piece honeydew melon
(optional)
250 ml/8 fl oz general household stock
made with chicken bones
2 spring onions
2–3 celery leaves
250 ml/8 fl oz pint tomato juice
a few drops Worcestershire sauce
3 cloves
a pinch of sugar
a few drops lemon juice
salt
cayenne pepper
15 ml/1 tbsp gelatine
30 ml/ 2 tbsp water*

Garnish
*45 ml/3 tbsp soured cream
freshly ground black pepper*

Remove the seeds from the melon, if using, and scoop out the flesh with a ball scoop. Chill the melon balls and the chicken stock while preparing the other ingredients.

Chop the onions finely and shred the celery leaves. Put into a large saucepan with the tomato juice, Worcestershire sauce, cloves, sugar, and lemon juice. Season to taste, half cover, and simmer for 10 minutes. Remove from the heat and strain into a bowl.

Soften the gelatine in the water in a small heatproof basin. Stand the basin in a pan of hot water and stir until it has dissolved. Add a little of the strained tomato liquid and stir well. Pour the gelatine into the remaining tomato liquid and mix well. Add the chilled chicken stock, stir until well blended, and leave to set.

To serve, whisk the jellied soup until frothy. Spoon into four chilled bowls, and gently mix in the melon balls, if using. Garnish with the soured cream and black pepper.

SERVES 4

FOLDING NAPKINS

Napkins look very pretty rolled and slipped into decorative rings. Alternatively, tie in place with narrow, satin ribbons that match the colour scheme, or simply fold into neat triangles, lay on side plates and add a single flower.

To fold napkins into decorative shapes, they must be at least 40 cm 16 in square. They need to be lightly starched and crisply ironed. These diagrams show two methods of folding. Place a flower in the centre of the Rose and Star, while the centre of the Mitre is an ideal place for warm bread rolls.

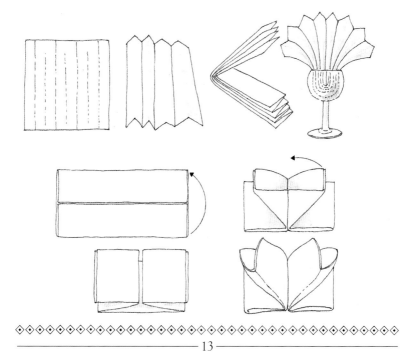

ROAST BEEF

Beef is the most popular joint for a roast lunch. Serve it with Yorkshire pudding and rich gravy made with the juices that have escaped during cooking.

ROAST BEEF

*a joint of beef suitable for roasting
salt and pepper
beef dripping (about 25 g/1 oz per
500 g/18 oz meat)*

Select the method of roasting, and weigh the meat to calculate the cooking time. Set the oven at the required temperature.

Wipe, trim, and tie the meat into a neat shape with fine string. Place the joint, fat side up, on a wire rack if available, in a shallow roasting tin. Season the meat, and rub or spread it with the dripping. Place the roasting tin in the oven and cook for the required time.

Transfer the cooked meat to a warmed serving dish, remove the string and secure with a metal skewer if necessary. Keep hot. Drain off the fat from the roasting tin and make a gravy from the sediment in the tin, if liked.

Serve with Yorkshire Pudding and Cold Horseradish Cream if using traditional accompaniments.

BASIC THIN BATTER

100 g/4 oz plain flour
1.25 ml/¼ tsp salt
1 egg
250 ml/8 fl oz milk

Sift the flour and salt into a bowl, make a well in the centre and add the egg. Stir in half the milk, gradually working the flour down from the sides. Beat vigorously until the mixture is smooth and bubbly. Stir in the remaining milk. Use to make Yorkshire Pudding or Individual Yorkshire Puddings.

MAKES ABOUT
375 ml/13 fl oz

YORKSHIRE PUDDING

Set the oven at 220°C/425°F/gas 7. Put 25 g/1 oz cooking fat, preferably beef dripping for flavour, or 25 ml/ 5 tsp oil into a 28 × 18 cm/7 × 11 inch baking tin. Heat in the oven for 15 minutes.

Remove the tin from the oven, pour in the basic thin batter quickly, and bake for 30–35 minutes, until well risen and brown in colour.

In the north of England, beef is cooked on a grid placed in the roasting tin. When the joint is basted for the last time, 30 minutes before it is cooked, the batter is poured into the tin below the grid, to cook in the meat dripping.

COLD HORSERADISH CREAM

125 ml/4½ fl oz double cream
30 ml/2 tbsp fresh grated horseradish
15 ml/1 tbsp white vinegar or lemon juice
10 ml/2 tsp caster sugar
1.25 ml/¼ tsp prepared English mustard
salt and pepper

Whip the cream lightly in a bowl until semi-stiff. Carefully fold in the other ingredients. Chill until ready to serve with beef.

MAKES ABOUT
150 ml/¼ pints

THIN GRAVY

pan juices
250 ml/8 fl oz hot water from cooking
vegetables
salt and pepper
(optional)
gravy browning
(optional)

After roasting a joint of beef,
carefully pour off the fat from the
roasting tin, leaving all the pan
juices and sediment behind. Add
the vegetable water or beef stock to
the juices. Bring to the boil,
stirring well until all the sediment
dissolves, and boil for 2–3 minutes
to reduce the liquid slightly. Season
to taste. If the gravy is too pale, add
a few drops of gravy browning.
Strain, and serve very hot with
roast beef.

MAKES ABOUT
250 ml/8 fl oz

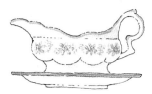

FILLET OF BEEF EN CROÛTE

800 g–1 kg/1¾–2¼ lb fillet of beef
ground pepper
15 ml/1 tbsp oil
25 g/1 oz butter
100 g/4 oz button mushrooms, sliced
5 ml/1 tsp chopped fresh mixed herbs
5 ml/1 tsp chopped parsley
450 g/1 lb prepared puff pastry
flour for rolling out
beaten egg for glazing

Set the oven at 230°C, 450°F, gas
8. Wipe, trim, and tie the meat
into a neat shape with fine string.
Season with pepper.

Heat the oil and butter in a large
saucepan, add the fillet and brown
it quickly all over. Reserve the fat
in the pan and draw it off the heat.
Transfer the fillet to a roasting tin
and roast for 10 minutes. Remove
the fillet, and leave it to get cold.

Meanwhile, sauté the
mushrooms in the remaining oil
and butter in the pan for 2–3
minutes. Remove from the heat,
add the herbs, and leave to cool.

Set the oven at 220°C/425°F/
gas 7. Roll out the puff pastry on a
lightly floured surface to make a
rectangle large enough to enclose

the fillet. Spread the mushroom mixture over one half of the pastry. Lay the beef on top of the mushroom mixture. Wrap the pastry round the beef to form a neat parcel, sealing the edges well.

Put the parcel on a baking sheet with the cut edges underneath. Garnish with leaves cut from the pastry trimmings and brush the pastry with the beaten egg. Bake for 20–30 minutes, or until the pastry is well-browned. Serve hot or cold.

SERVES 6

SELECTING GOOD MEAT

Beef – look for red, marbled meat with as little fat as possible; any fat should be a pale creamy colour, and the meat should be firm and elastic and scarcely moisten the fingers.

Veal – choose white or very pale pink, firm meat with bubbly tissue between the muscles; any fat should be firm and white.

Mutton – fresh meat should be a cherry red and firmer than beef; fat should be white, firm and waxy; if the flesh remains creased when pinched it is old and will be tough.

Lamb – look for lean, firm meat with pearly, white fat.

Pork – this should be smooth, firm and pale pink with firm fat and a smooth, thin rind; reject all meat with a tinge of red.

Ham – choose a ham that does not have too much fat, and what fat there is should be white, not yellow; the lean should not be too dark or too soft.

Poultry – the flesh should be firm and thick, look for small-boned, plump birds with some fat; the breast bone, wing tips and feet should be pliable, the legs smooth and the skin white and soft. Frozen poultry must be completely thawed before cooking.

MRS BEETON'S ROAST RIBS OF BEEF

2.5 kg/5½ lb forerib of beef
flour for dredging
50–75 g/2–3 oz clarified dripping
*(see **Note**)*
salt and pepper
shredded horseradish
to garnish

Ask the butcher to trim the thin ends of the rib bones so that the joint will stand upright.

Set the oven at 230°C/450°F/ gas 8. Wipe the meat but do not salt it. Dredge it lightly with flour.

Melt 50 g/2 oz of the dripping in a roasting tin and brush some of it over the meat. Put the meat in the tin and roast it in the oven for 10 minutes. Baste well, reduce temperature to 180°C/350°F/gas **4**, and continue to roast for 1¾ hours for rare meat, or 2¼ hours for well-done meat. Baste frequently during cooking, using extra dripping if required.

When cooked, salt the meat lightly. Transfer the joint to a warmed serving dish and keep hot.

Pour off almost all the fat in the roasting tin, leaving the sediment.

Pour in enough water to make a thin gravy, then heat to boiling point, stirring all the time. Taste, and season with salt and pepper. Strain the gravy into a warmed gravy-boat.

Garnish the dish with one or two small heaps of shredded horseradish.

Note To clarify dripping, put the dripping into a large saucepan and add about the same volume of cold water. Heat very gently until the water begins to boil, removing the scum as it rises. Allow to simmer for about 5 minutes, then strain into a bowl and leave to cool and solidify. Remove the fat in one piece, dry it on absorbent kitchen paper and scrape away the sediment from underneath. Heat the fat very slowly until all bubbling ceases, to drive off any water.

SERVES 6–8

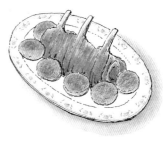

MARINATED ROAST BEEF

*800 g–1 kg/1¾–2¼ lb fillet **or** boned*
*sirloin **or** topside of beef*
fat for greasing
250 ml/8 fl oz Demi-glace Sauce

Marinade
30 ml/2 tbsp olive oil
*15 ml/1 tbsp lemon juice **or** vinegar*
5 ml/1 tsp chopped onion
5 ml/1 tsp chopped parsley
a pinch of dried mixed herbs
a pinch of ground cloves
a pinch of ground pepper
1.25 ml/¼ tsp salt

Make the marinade first by mixing all the ingredients together. Wipe, trim, and tie the meat into a neat shape with fine string. Put the meat in a mixing bowl, pour the marinade over and leave it to soak for 2–3 hours, turning and basting frequently.

Set the oven at 190°C/375°F/gas 5. Cut a sheet of foil large enough to form a parcel round the meat, and grease it well. Lay the foil in an ovenproof dish with sides so that it forms a container, and place the meat in the centre. Pour the marinade over the meat.

Fold the foil lightly round the meat and seal the edges to form a loose parcel. Roast the beef for 1 hour for fillet, and 1½ hours for sirloin or topside. Open the foil for the last 15 minutes of the cooking time to let the meat brown.

Lift out the meat, place it on a warmed serving dish and remove the string. Brush with Demi-glace Sauce. If liked, a little of the sauce can also be poured round the dish, the rest being served separately. Serve with Cold Horseradish Cream.

SERVES 6–8

ROAST PORK

Small-boned lean pork is best for roasting. Rub the skin with dry mustard powder before roasting for a really crispy result to your crackling.

ROAST PORK

a joint of pork on the bone suitable for roasting
salt and pepper
oil or fat for basting

Ask the butcher to score the rind in narrow lines, or do it yourself with a sharp knife. Select the method of roasting, and weigh the joint to calculate the cooking time. Set the oven at the required temperature.

Wipe the meat. Place the joint on a rack in a shallow roasting tin. Season the meat with salt and pepper, and pour over a little oil or rub it with a little fat. Rub some salt into the scored rind to produce crisp crackling. Place the roasting tin in the oven, and cook for the required time.

If liked, brush the joint with smooth apricot jam or glaze with syrup from canned peaches, 10 minutes before the end of the cooking time. Alternatively, sprinkle the rind with brown sugar mixed with a little mustard powder. These mixtures give a sweeter crisp crackling. If a non-sweet glaze is wanted for the crackling, brush the joint with lightly salted butter or oil, with a little extra salt added. Raise the oven heat for a short time to crispen the crackling.

Transfer the cooked meat to a warmed meat dish and keep hot. Prepare the thickened gravy from the sediment in the roasting tin.

Serve roast pork with sage and onion stuffing balls and apple sauce accompaniments.

ROAST BONED, STUFFED PORK

1.5 kg/3½ lb boned bladebone of pork
45 ml/3 tbsp oil

Stuffing
*25 g/1 oz butter **or** margarine*
1 onion, finely chopped
1 celery stick, finely chopped
100 g/4 oz flat mushrooms,
finely chopped
*50 g/2 oz canned **or** frozen sweetcorn*
50 g/2 oz white breadcrumbs
15 ml/1 tbsp chopped parsley
salt and pepper
2.5 ml/½ tsp ground mace
5ml/1 tsp lemon juice

Set the oven at 200°C/400°F/gas 6.

Wipe the meat and deeply score the rind of the meat if not done by the butcher.

Make the stuffing. Melt the butter or margarine in a small pan and fry the onion and celery until lightly browned. Remove from the heat. Add the mushrooms, sweetcorn, breadcrumbs and parsley, and mix well. Season to taste, and add the mace and lemon juice.

Spoon the stuffing evenly into the 'pocket' left after the meat was boned. Roll up the joint and tie with thin string at regular intervals.

Heat 30 ml/2 tbsp of the oil in a roasting tin, then put in the joint. Brush the rind with the remaining oil and sprinkle generously with salt.

Roast in the oven for 20–30 minutes, until the crackling is browned. Reduce the temperature to 180°C/350°F/gas 4 and continue to cook for 1½ hours or until the internal temperature reaches 85–88°C/185–190°F on a meat thermometer.

Transfer the joint to a warmed serving dish, remove the string, and keep the meat hot. Pour off the fat in the roasting tin, then prepare a gravy using the sediment left in the tin.

SERVES 6

21

SAGE AND ONION STUFFING

2 small onions, thickly sliced
4 young sage leaves **or** *2.5 ml/½ tsp*
dried sage
100 g/4 oz soft white breadcrumbs
50 g/2 oz butter **or** *margarine*
salt and pepper
1 egg (optional)

Put the onions in a saucepan with a little water and parboil. Drain and chop the onions finely. Scald the fresh sage leaves, if used, and chop them finely. Mix together with the onions and breadcrumbs. Melt the butter or margarine, add to the stuffing, and season to taste. Mix together thoroughly. Use as described in recipes.

If the stuffing is to be shaped into balls, beat the egg until liquid and add enough to the stuffing to bind it. Place on a baking sheet, and bake at 180°C/350°F/gas 4 for 15–20 minutes. Alternatively, fry in deep or shallow fat until golden.

APPLE SAUCE

500 g/18 oz apples, sliced
30 ml/2 tbsp water
15 g/½ oz butter **or** *margarine*
rind and juice of ½ lemon
sugar

Put the apples into a saucepan with the water, fat, and lemon rind. Cover, and cook over low heat until the apple is reduced to a pulp, then purée. Reheat the sauce with the lemon juice and sugar to taste.

Serve hot or cold with roast pork, duck or goose.

MAKES ABOUT
375 ml/13 fl oz

THICKENED GRAVY

pan juices
15 ml/1 tbsp plain flour
250 ml/8 fl oz hot water from cooking
vegetables **or** *general household stock*
made with pork meat
trimmings and vegetables
salt and pepper
(optional)

After roasting a joint, pour off most

of the fat from the roasting tin, leaving 30 ml/2 tbsp of fat and sediment in the tin. Sift the flour over the fat, and blend thoroughly with the pan juices. Stir and cook gently until browned. Gradually add the hot liquid, and stir until boiling. Boil for 3–4 minutes. Season to taste. Strain, and serve very hot with roast pork.

MAKES ABOUT
250 ml/8 fl oz

4. Wipe the meat and weigh it to calculate the cooking time.

Spread the prunes over the flesh; roll up the meat and secure with fine string. Pour the lemon juice over the joint and rub it in well.

Melt the lard or butter in a roasting tin, put in the joint, season with salt and pepper, and baste. Roast in the oven, and baste occasionally.

Serve on a warmed dish and accompany with a thickened gravy (page 22) made from the sediment in the roasting tin. Garnish with stewed prunes, if liked.

SERVES 6

ROAST PORK STUFFED WITH PRUNES

200 g/7 oz prunes
1.25–1.5 kg/2¾–3½ lb boned loin of pork
juice of 1 lemon
*25 g/1 oz lard **or** butter*
salt and pepper

Cover the prunes with boiling water and soak them for 2 hours. Drain, and remove the stones.

Set the oven at 180°C/350°F/gas

ℛOAST LAMB

Lamb used to be a traditional spring dish for festive occasions. It is now more readily available all the year round than mutton. Serve the meat with fresh mint sauce, mint jelly or redcurrant jelly.

ROAST LEG OF LAMB

*a leg of lamb **or** mutton
salt and pepper
oil **or** fat for basting*

Set the oven at 230°C/450°F/gas 8.

Weigh the meat to calculate the cooking time, allowing 20 minutes per 500 g/1 lb plus 20 minutes extra.

Wipe the meat. Place the leg on a wire rack, if available, in a shallow roasting tin. Season the meat, and either pour over a little oil or rub it with a little fat. Place the roasting tin in the oven, and cook for about 10 minutes to sear or brown the outside of the meat and seal in the juices. Reduce the temperature to 190°C/375°F/gas 5 to finish the cooking.

Transfer the cooked meat from the oven to a warmed meat dish, and keep hot. Prepare a gravy, if liked, from the sediment in the roasting tin.

Serve with mint sauce.

SERVES 6

STUFFED ROAST SHOULDER OF LAMB OR MUTTON

*a shoulder of lamb **or** mutton*
salt and pepper
*150–200 g/5–7 oz basic herb **or** sage and onion (page 25 **or** page 22) stuffing*
dripping

Set the oven at 180°C/350°F/gas 4.

Remove all the bones from the meat. Wipe the meat and trim off any skin and excess fat. Flatten the meat with a cutlet bat or rolling pin. Season the inner surface of the meat well with salt and pepper and spread on the stuffing. Roll the meat up and secure with fine string.

Weigh the meat to calculate the cooking time.

Heat the dripping in a roasting tin, put in the meat, and baste with the dripping. Cover the roasting tin loosely with foil and roast the meat until tender. Baste occasionally during the cooking time.

Serve on a warmed dish with gravy made from the meat juices.

SERVES 6–10

BASIC HERB STUFFING

*50 g/2 oz shredded suet **or** margarine*
100 g/4 oz soft breadcrumbs
a pinch of grated nutmeg
15 ml/1 tbsp chopped parsley
5 ml/1 tsp chopped fresh mixed herbs
grated rind of ½ lemon
salt and pepper
1 egg, lightly beaten

Melt the margarine, if using. Mix the breadcrumbs with the suet or margarine in a bowl. Add the nutmeg, herbs, and lemon rind. Season with salt and pepper. Stir the egg into the mixture to bind it.

Use for chicken, lamb, veal, fish or vegetables. Alternatively, form the mixture into 12 or 16 balls, and bake at 180°C/350°F/gas 4 for 15–20 minutes, or fry in deep or shallow fat until golden.

MINT JELLY

*1 kg/2¼ lb green apples, unpeeled and
quartered
500 ml/17 fl oz water
a small bunch of fresh mint
500 ml/17 fl oz vinegar
sugar (see recipe)
about 45 ml/3 tbsp chopped mint
a few drops green colouring (optional)*

Put the apples in a preserving pan
with the water and the bunch of
mint. Simmer until the apples are
soft and pulpy, then add the
vinegar and boil for 5 minutes.
Strain the pulp through a scalded
jelly bag and leave the residue to
drip for 1–2 hours.

Measure the juice and return it
to the cleaned pan. Add 800 g/1¾
lb sugar for each litre/1¾ pints of
juice, and bring to the boil, stirring
all the time until the sugar is
dissolved. Boil rapidly for about 25
minutes, without stirring, until
setting point is nearly reached, add
the chopped mint and colouring, if
used, then boil steadily until setting
point is reached. Test by putting a
spoonful on a cold saucer.

Remove from the heat, fill into
warmed jars and cover
immediately. Label and store.

MINT SAUCE

*60 ml/4 tbsp chopped fresh mint
10 ml/2 tsp sugar
15 ml/1 tbsp boiling water
30 ml/2 tbsp vinegar*

Put the mint into a sauce-boat.
Sprinkle with the sugar. Add the
boiling water, and stir until the
sugar dissolves; then add the
vinegar. Leave the sauce for 1–2
hours for the flavours to infuse.
Serve with roast lamb.

MAKES ABOUT
125 ml/4½ fl oz

LAMB GRAVY

*pan juices
5 ml/1 tsp plain flour
250 ml/8 fl oz hot water from
vegetables **or** general household stock
made with lamb meat trimmings and
vegetables
salt and pepper
(optional)
gravy browning
(optional)*

Make as for Thin Gravy but, after

pouring off the fat, stir the flour into the pan juices. Add the hot vegetable water or stock gradually to prevent lumps forming, and stir until boiling. Season to taste, if required. If the gravy is too pale, add a few drops of gravy browning. Strain, and serve very hot with roast lamb.

MAKES ABOUT
250 ml/8 fl oz

❖❖❖❖❖❖❖❖❖❖❖❖❖❖❖❖❖❖❖❖❖❖❖❖❖❖❖❖❖❖❖❖

ACCOMPANIMENTS

Apple sauce
Apple sauce has for many years been a favourite accompaniment to all pork dishes. This could well be because windfalls needed using in the autumn at the same time as the family pig was slaughtered for winter food.

Horseradish sauce
Horseradish sauce or creamed horseradish has for centuries been a popular accompaniment to roast beef. The plant is native to Eastern Europe and also grows well in Britain, particularly in wet ground. Most of its pungency is in the outer part of the root and it loses its flavour rapidly if allowed to dry. It is usually grated and mixed with vinegar or cream and is also very good with fish and salads of chicken, eggs and tomatoes.

Mint sauce
Mint and mint sauce were introduced to Britain by the Romans, and they have traditionally been used to accompany lamb and mutton. Mint is also extremely good with potatoes, peas, beans, lentils, duck, oranges, cucumber, tomatoes, aubergines, carrots and mushrooms.

Redcurrant jelly
Since the earliest times, redcurrants have been served with mutton and venison. In venison stews and with hare, port is usually also added. Similar jellies may be made with barberries and rowanberries.

❖❖❖❖❖❖❖❖❖❖❖❖❖❖❖❖❖❖❖❖❖❖❖❖❖❖❖❖❖❖❖❖

REDCURRANT JELLY

2 kg/4¼ lb large, juicy redcurrants or redcurrants and white currants mixed
sugar (see recipe)

Remove the leaves and the larger stems, and wash the fruit if necessary. Put the fruit in a preserving pan, without any water, and heat very gently for about 45 minutes or until the currants are softened and well cooked.

Mash with a wooden spoon, then strain the pulp through a scalded jelly bag. Leave it to drip for 1 hour.

Measure the extract, and return it to the cleaned pan. Add 1 kg/2¼ lb sugar for each litre/1¾ pints of extract. Bring to the boil, stirring all the time, then boil, without stirring, for 1 minute. Skim the jelly quickly, and immediately pour it into warmed jars, before it has a chance to set in the pan. Cover and label with name and date.

The above recipe, using undiluted fruit juice, makes a good full-flavoured jelly. For less experienced cooks, it is easier to add enough water to cover the fruit and to make two extractions and then mix them; add 800 g/1¾ lb sugar for each litre/1¾ pints of extract. This will give a larger yield of slightly less robust-flavoured jelly, but it will not set before there is time to pour it into pots.

CROWN ROAST OF LAMB WITH SAFFRON RICE

2 best ends of neck of lamb (6 cutlets each)
oil for brushing
salt and pepper

Saffron Rice
500 ml/17 fl oz general household stock made from chicken bones
1.25 ml/¼ tsp powdered saffron
50 g/2 oz butter
1 celery stick, chopped
1 onion, chopped
150 g/5 oz long-grain white rice
60 ml/4 tbsp dry white wine
25 g/1 oz blanched almonds, chopped
2 dessert apples, diced
50g /2 oz frozen green peas

Set the oven at 190°C/375°F/gas 5.
Ask the butcher to prepare the crown roast or prepare it as follows.

Wipe the meat. Remove the fat and meat from the top 5 cm/ 2 inches of the thin ends of the bones and scrape the bone ends clean with a sharp knife. Slice the lower half of each best end of neck between each bone, about two-thirds up from the base. Trim off any excess fat.

Turn the joints so that the bones are on the outside and the meat is on the inside, and sew the pieces together with a trussing needle and fine string. The thick ends of the meat will form the base of the crown, so ensure they are level.

Place the prepared crown roast in a roasting tin. Brush it with oil and season well. Wrap a piece of foil round the top of each cutlet bone to prevent it from scorching. Cook for 1¼–1½ hours.

About 30 minutes before the end of the cooking time, make the saffron rice. Heat the stock in a saucepan with the powdered saffron. Heat 25 g/1 oz of the butter in another saucepan and fry the celery and onion gently until softened but not browned.

Wash the rice, stir it into the vegetables and cook for 1–2 minutes. Pour on the wine and cook gently until the rice has absorbed it. Add 250 ml/8 fl oz of the hot stock and cook, uncovered, stirring occasionally, until almost all the liquid is absorbed. Pour the remaining stock into the rice and cook gently until it has been completely absorbed and the rice is just tender.

Remove the rice from the heat and add the almonds, diced apple, peas, and remaining butter. Cover the pan with a tight-fitting lid, and leave to cook in its own steam off the heat until the peas are thawed and heated through, and the roast is ready.

When cooked, place the crown roast on a warmed serving dish. Remove the foil from the cutlet bones. Fill the hollow centre of the roast with the hot saffron rice. Top each cutlet with a cutlet frill and serve. Any extra rice can be served separately.

SERVES 6

VEAL

Although veal may be bought all the year round it is most plentiful in spring and summer. It is expensive but quite delicious and lighter than beef.

STUFFED BREAST OF VEAL

a thick end of breast of veal
(1 kg/2¼ lb approx)
salt and pepper
300 g/10 oz pork sausagemeat
1 large onion
1 large carrot
½ turnip
bouquet garni
6 black peppercorns
water to cover
butter for greasing
250 g/8 oz short-grain rice
50 g/2 oz grated Parmesan cheese
lemon slices to garnish

Remove all bones and tendons from the meat. Wipe, then season well. Spread the sausagemeat evenly over the inner surface of the meat, roll up and tie securely with fine string.

Prepare and slice the vegetables.

Put them with the bones and trimmings in a large pan. Add the bouquet garni, peppercorns, salt and pepper, and enough water to cover the vegetables. Place the meat on top, cover with buttered greaseproof paper and a tight-fitting lid.

Heat to boiling point, reduce the heat and simmer gently for about 2½ hours. Baste occasionally and add more water if necessary. Keep meat hot in a warmed dish.

Strain off the liquid and make it up to 750 ml/1¼ pints with water. Put the stock in a pan and bring to the boil. Wash the rice and cook it in the stock until the stock is absorbed. Season to taste and stir in the cheese.

Place the rice in a layer on a warmed serving dish and put the meat on top. Garnish with lemon slices.

SERVES 6

$\mathcal{H}$AM

Baked or boiled ham makes a very tasty change from other meats and it is excellent served cold.

HAM WITH RAISIN SAUCE

1.5–2 kg/3½–4½ lb parboiled York ham
250 g/9 oz dark soft brown sugar
cloves
100 ml/4 fl oz white wine vinegar

Raisin Sauce
50 g/2 oz soft dark brown sugar
2.5 ml/½ tsp English mustard
15 ml/1 tbsp cornflour
75 g/3 oz seedless raisins
15 ml/1 tbsp grated orange rind
100 ml/4 fl oz fresh orange juice
200 ml/7 fl oz water

Set the oven at 160°C/325°F/gas 3.

Put the ham in a shallow baking tin and bake, uncovered, in the oven for 10 minutes per 500 g/18 oz meat.

Thirty minutes before the end of cooking time, lift out the meat and remove the rind. Score the fat in a pattern of diamonds. Cover the fat with brown sugar and press in cloves at the points of the diamond pattern. Trickle the wine vinegar gently over the ham. Continue baking, basting with the juices, until the ham is fully cooked.

Make the Raisin Sauce. Mix together in a saucepan the brown sugar, mustard and cornflour. Add the rest of the ingredients and cook very gently for 10 minutes or until sauce is of a syrupy consistency.

Transfer the cooked ham to a warmed serving dish and serve the sauce separately in a sauce-boat.

SERVES 8–10

$\mathscr{C}$HICKEN

Chicken is one of the most cheapest meats on the market today, and therefore makes an economical but very tempting meal. Serve with traditional stuffings, bread sauce and cranberry jelly.

ROAST CHICKEN

1 roasting chicken
oil or fat for basting
salt and pepper
2-3 rashers streaky bacon (optional)
15 ml/1 tbsp plain flour
275 ml/9 fl oz general household stock made with chicken bones
gravy browning

Set the oven at the required temperature (see chart on page 34). Truss the chicken if liked.

Put the oil or fat in a roasting tin and place for a few minutes in the oven. Remove from the oven.

Place the chicken in the roasting tin, on a trivet if liked. Baste with the oil or fat, sprinkle with salt and pepper, and lay the bacon rashers, if used, over the breast. Cover the breast with a piece of foil or buttered greaseproof paper, if liked.

Return the tin to the oven and cook the bird for the recommended time until tender. (Prick the thigh to test for tenderness; if there is any trace of blood, the chicken is not cooked.) The bacon and foil or greaseproof paper should be removed 10-15 minutes before serving, to allow the breast to brown.

When cooked, place the chicken on a hot carving dish, remove trussing strings or skewers, and keep hot. Pour off and discard the excess fat from the tin, keeping back the sediment for gravy. Sprinkle in the flour, stir well with a metal spoon, and add the stock gradually. Bring to the boil and boil for about 2-3 minutes. Season to taste, add a little gravy browning, and strain into a hot sauce-boat. Alternatively, the gravy can be made with the giblets (page 34).

Serve with the traditional accompaniments of bacon rolls (page 35), balls made with basic herb stuffing (page 25) and bread sauce. Add watercress garnishes.

SERVES 4–6

CELEBRATION
LUNCH
AL FRESCO

stuffed tomato salad

*chicken in cider and
cream sauce
bacon rolls
roast potatoes
glazed carrots
steamed cauliflower*

*summer pudding with whipped
cream
Mrs Beeton's Charlotte Russe*

ROAST CHICKEN WITH HONEY AND ALMONDS

1 roasting chicken
½ lemon
salt and pepper
45 ml/3 tbsp honey
50 g/2 oz blanched almonds
a pinch of powdered saffron (optional)
30 ml/2 tbsp oil

Set the oven at 180–190°C/ 350–375°F/gas 4–5.

Truss the chicken. Rub all over with the cut lemon, then sprinkle with salt and pepper. Line a roasting tin with a piece of foil large enough to cover the bird and to meet over the top. Put the bird on the foil, and rub it all over with honey. Slice the almonds and sprinkle them and the saffron, if used, over the bird. Pour the oil over the bird very gently. Wrap it completely in the foil, keeping it clear of the skin. Seal by folding over the edges. Roast in the oven for about 1½ hours, until tender. Unwrap the foil for the last 10 minutes to allow the breast to brown.

SERVES 4–6

ROASTING POULTRY

Approximate cooking times:

weight	unstuffed or with neck end only stuffed, at at 160°C/325°F/gas 3	fully stuffed, at 180°C/350°F/gas 4 (after 20 minutes at 200°C/400°F/gas 6)
2.5 kg/5½ lb	2½–3 hours	2½–3 hours
2.75–3.5 kg/6–8 lb	3–3¼ hours	3–3¼ hours
3.5–4.5 kg/8–10 lb	3½–4 hours	3¼–4½ hours
4.5–5.5 kg/10–12 lb	4–4½ hours	4½–5 hours
5.5–13.5 kg/12–30 lb	20 minutes per 500 g/18 oz + 20 minutes	20 minutes per 500 g/18 oz + 20 minutes

GIBLET GRAVY

1 set of giblets
1 onion (optional)
400 ml/14 fl oz water
pan juices
gravy browning (optional)
salt and pepper (optional)

If bought from a poulterer or obtained with a frozen bird, the giblets are ready prepared for cooking. If using giblets from a bird bought before eviscerating, cut the small greenish gall-bladder away from the liver, taking care not to break it; it will give the giblets a very bitter flavour. Cut any small sinews from the liver, and cut excess fat off the heart and gizzard. Break the neck into two or three pieces. Rinse the giblets in cold water if necessary.

Put the prepared giblets and the onion in a saucepan and cover with cold water. Heat to boiling point, cover, reduce the heat, and simmer gently for 1 hour.

Pour off the fat from the tin in which the bird has been roasted, leaving any sediment. Add the liquid from the giblets and stir until boiling. Boil for 2-3 minutes. If the gravy is too pale, add a few drops of gravy browning. Season to taste, if required. Strain and serve very hot with roast poultry.

The gravy can be thickened slightly, if liked, by adding 5 ml/1 tsp plain flour for each 250 ml/8 fl oz giblet stock. Blend the flour with the sediment before adding the stock. Boil for 3-4 minutes.

MAKES ABOUT
300 ml/¹/₂ pints

BACON ROLLS

Trim away the rinds of streaky bacon. Roll up each rasher. If frying, secure the outer end with a wooden toothpick inserted along each roll. If grilling, thread on short metal skewers.

Put the prepared rashers in a dry frying pan or under moderate grilling heat, and fry or grill for 3-5 minutes, turning frequently, for a crisp effect.

◇◇

CARVING

For successful carving it is most important to have a sharp knife. The cuts should be direct, sharp and incisive. It is also very important that the joint is served on a plate that is big enough to give the carver ample room for manoeuvre.

Meat is usually cut across the grain except with a saddle of lamb or mutton, which is carved at right angles to the rib bones.

Here are some hints for the more difficult joints of meat:

Ribs of beef – cut slices off the side, starting at the thick end and cutting through to the other end.

Leg of pork – cut down to the bone and run the knife between bone and meat to ease the slices out.

Loin of pork – always ensure the crackling is well scored.

Leg of lamb – start in the middle and cut down to the bone.

Chicken – insert the fork into the breast and cut down between the body and the thigh. Detach the leg by twisting the knife. Remove the wings, lifting off with them some of the breast meat. Slice the breast.

◇◇

$\mathscr{V}$EGETABLES

*Choose vegetables that offer a contrast in colour and
texture to the joint. Steam or lightly boil them so that they
retain their goodness, flavour and crispness.*

ROAST POTATOES

Set the oven at 190°–220°C/375–
425°F/gas5–7.

Cut old potatoes into even-sized
pieces (halves or quarters). Put in a
saucepan of boiled salted water,
parboil for 5 minutes, and drain
thoroughly. Return the potatoes to
the pan and stand over low heat for
1-2 minutes, shaking the pan
occasionally, until the potatoes are
quite dry.

Heat a little lard or dripping in a
roasting tin, add the potatoes, and
turn in the fat so that they are
evenly coated, or put the potatoes
in the dripping around a joint of
roast meat.

Roast for 40 minutes to 1 hour,
or until crisp and golden brown.
Baste the potatoes with some of the
fat several times during cooking.
The cooking time will vary

according to the size of the potatoes
and the oven temperature, which
will depend on the type of joint
being roasted. Parboiling helps to
give a very crisp roast potato.

Alternatively, cut the potatoes
into even-sized pieces. Put into a
roasting tin containing hot
dripping or fat, coat evenly with
fat, and roast as above for
1-1¼ hours depending on the size
of the potatoes and the oven
temperature.

ANNA POTATOES

fat for greasing
1 kg/2¼ lb even-sized potatoes
salt and pepper
melted clarified butter **or** *margarine*

Thoroughly grease a 20 cm/8 inch round cake tin and line the base with greased greaseproof paper. Set the oven at 190°C/375°F/gas 5.

Trim the potatoes so that they will give equal-sized slices. Slice them very thinly using either a sharp knife or a mandoline. Arrange a layer of potatoes, slightly overlapping, in the base of the prepared tin. Season, and spoon a little clarified fat over them. Make a second layer of potatoes, season, and spoon some more fat over them. Complete these layers, until all the potatoes have been used.

Cover the tin with greased greaseproof paper and foil. Bake for 1 hour. Check the potatoes several times during cooking and add a little more clarified fat if they become too dry. Uncover for the last 15 minutes to brown.

Invert the tin on to a warmed serving dish to remove the potatoes, and serve immediately.

SERVES 6

ROAST PARSNIPS

Set the oven at 190°–200°C/375–400°F/gas 5–6.

Cut the parsnips into quarters lengthways. Put in a saucepan of boiling salted water, and parboil for 10 minutes. Drain and dry thoroughly with absorbent kitchen paper.

Heat a little dripping in a roasting tin. Add the parsnips and roll in the hot dripping. Alternatively, put the parsnips into the dripping in a pan around a roast joint. Roast for 45 minutes to 1 hour, or until tender and golden brown.

COURGETTES WITH TOMATOES

30 ml/2 tbsp olive oil
500 g/18 oz courgettes, sliced
6 spring onions, chopped
1 clove garlic, crushed
200 g/7 oz tomatoes
15 ml/1 tbsp concentrated tomato
purée
1 bay leaf
15 ml/1 tbsp chopped basil
30 ml/2 tbsp white wine
salt and pepper

Heat the oil in a frying pan, add the courgettes, spring onions, and garlic, and cook for 5 minutes, stirring occasionally.

Peel the tomatoes, cut in half, and remove the pips. Add to the courgette mixture with the tomato purée, bay leaf, basil, white wine, and seasoning. Bring to the boil, cover, and simmer gently for 15 minutes.

SERVES 4

GLAZED CARROTS

675 g/1½ lb young carrots
50 g/2 oz butter
3 sugar lumps
2.5 ml/¼ tsp salt
beef stock
15 ml/1 tbsp chopped parsley
to garnish

Prepare the carrots but leave them whole. Heat the butter in a saucepan. Add the carrots, sugar, salt, and enough stock to half cover the carrots. Cook gently, without a lid for 15-20 minutes or until the carrots are tender, shaking the pan occasionally.

Remove the carrots with a perforated spoon and keep warm. Boil the stock rapidly in the pan until it is reduced to a rich glaze. Replace the carrots, 2–3 at a time, and turn them in the glaze until they are thoroughly coated. Place on a serving dish and garnish with parsley before serving.

SERVES 6

LEEKS IN PARMESAN SAUCE

1 kg/2¼ lb leeks
1 litre/1¾ pints water
10 ml/2 tsp salt
*25 g/1 oz butter **or** margarine*
25 g/1 oz plain flour
300 ml/½ pint well-flavoured vegetable stock
150 ml/¼ pint single cream
salt and pepper
a pinch of grated nutmeg
1 chicken stock cube
50 g/2 oz grated Parmesan cheese
15 ml/1 tbsp mixed chopped parsley and chives to garnish

Prepare the leeks and keep them whole; tie up in a bundle. Bring the water and salt to the boil in a saucepan and cook the leeks for 20 minutes, then drain well. Put to one side.

Meanwhile, melt the fat in a small pan, add the flour, and cook for about 4 minutes, stirring until the mixture looks like wet sand. Add the stock gradually, stirring all the time, to make a sauce. Bring to the boil, lower the heat, and stir until the mixture thickens. Stir in the cream, a little salt and simmer gently for 5 minutes. Crumble the stock cube into the sauce. Boil for 5 minutes longer.

Remove from the heat, and scatter in half the grated cheese. Untie the bundle of leeks. Put in a long, shallow, flameproof dish and cover with the sauce. Sprinkle with the remaining cheese, and brown under the grill for 5-6 minutes. Sprinkle the herbs on top just before serving.

SERVES 4

WINTER LUNCH

artichoke soup

fillet of beef en croute
gravy
horseradish sauce
roast potatoes
baked onions
courgettes with tomatoes
sprouts

queen of puddings
treacle tart

ITALIAN SPINACH

25 g/1 oz butter **or** *margarine*
1 kg/2¼ lb spinach
salt and pepper
25 g/1 oz sultanas
30 ml/2 tbsp olive oil
1 garlic clove, crushed
25 g/1 oz pine kernels

Melt the butter in a pan, add the wet spinach leaves, season with salt, then cover and cook slowly for about 10 minutes or until the spinach is tender. Drain thoroughly; then chop coarsely.

Cover the sultanas with boiling water for 1 minute to plump them; then drain thoroughly.

Heat the oil in a wide pan. Add the spinach, garlic, and seasoning. Turn the spinach over and over in the pan to heat it thoroughly without frying. Add the sultanas and nuts and serve hot.

SERVES 4

GLAZED ONIONS

400 g/14 oz button onions
chicken stock
salt and pepper
15 ml/1 tbsp light soft brown sugar
25 g/1 oz butter
a pinch of grated nutmeg

Put the onions in a saucepan in which they just fit in one layer. Add just enough stock to cover them. Heat to simmering point, and simmer for 15–20 minutes until the onions are just tender, adding a very little extra hot stock if needed. When the onions are ready, the stock should be reduced almost to a glaze.

Remove from the heat, and add the rest of the ingredients. Turn the onions over with a spoon to blend the extra seasonings well with the stock and to coat the onions. Return to the heat, and shake the onions in the pan, until the glaze and fat give them a shiny brown coating. Serve, at once, with the remaining syrupy glaze. **Note** Glazed onions are often used as a garnish.

SERVES 4

COOKING
VEGETABLES

Most people have today recognized the fact that by boiling vegetables for the number of minutes recommended by Victorian cookery writers, they lose not only their vital minerals and vitamins, but their taste too. Why not try other ways of cooking vegetables so that they retain their nutritional value, colour and flavour.

Steaming

Wash and peel the vegetables in the usual way, slice thinly and lay in a special steamer or in a bowl, with any herbs and seasoning, and place over a saucepan of boiling water for 5–10 minutes, depending on the size and thickness of the vegetables. Dense or hard vegetables such as sprouts or fennel will take longer than mange-tout or thinly sliced carrots.

Steaming in a microwave oven

Place the prepared vegetables in a bowl with any herbs and seasoning and about 30 ml/2 tbsp of cold water (spinach, mushrooms and leeks need no water). Cover and cook on high until they reach the desired texture (times will depend on quantities and the denseness of the individual vegetables).

Stir-frying

Heat a heavy pan or wok with a few drops of oil or butter, add the vegetables, herbs and seasoning, and cook, stirring all the time, for 4–5 minutes, or longer, to suit personal taste.

UDDINGS

*Sunday lunch would not be complete without a special
pudding. Serve a light fruit soufflé or creamy trifle in
summer, or draw cries of nostalgic delight from your guests
with a queen of puddings or treacle tart in winter.*

MRS BEETON'S BRANDY TRIFLE

1 × 15 cm/6 inch sponge cake
30 ml/2 tbsp redcurrant jelly
75 ml/3 fl oz brandy
50 g/2 oz whole blanched almonds
375 ml/13 fl oz milk
125 ml/4½ fl oz single cream
8 egg yolks
75 g/3 oz caster sugar
extra redcurrant jelly to decorate

Put the cake in a glass bowl or dish
16 cm/6½ inches in diameter and
as deep as the cake. Spread the
cake thinly with jelly, then pour
over as much brandy as the cake
can absorb.

Cut the almonds lengthways into
spikes and stick them all over the
top of the cake.

Mix the milk and cream in a
bowl. In a second, heatproof bowl,
beat the yolks until liquid, and pour
the milk and cream over them. Stir
in the sugar. Transfer the mixture
to the top of a double saucepan and
cook over gently simmering water
for about 10 minutes or until the
custard thickens, stirring all the
time. Let the custard cool slightly,
then pour it over and around the
cake. Cover with dampened
greaseproof paper.

When cold, refrigerate the trifle
for about 1 hour. Decorate with
small spoonfuls of redcurrant jelly
and serve.

SERVES 4–6

QUEEN OF PUDDINGS

75 g/3 oz soft white breadcrumbs
400 ml/14 fl oz milk
25 g/ 1 oz butter
10 ml/2 tsp grated lemon rind
2 eggs
75 g/3 oz caster sugar
fat for greasing
30 ml/2 tbsp red jam

Dry the breadcrumbs slightly by placing in a cool oven for a few moments. Warm the milk with the butter and lemon rind, to approximately 65°C/149°F; do not let it come near the boil.

Separate the eggs and stir 25 g/ 1 oz of the sugar into the yolks. Pour the warmed milk over the yolks, and stir in well. Add the crumbs and mix thoroughly. Pour the custard mixture into a greased 750 ml/1¼ pint pie dish and leave to stand for 30 minutes.

Set the oven at 160°C/325°F/ gas 3. Bake the pudding for 40–45 minutes until it is lightly set. Remove the pudding from the oven and reduce the temperature to 120°C/250°F/gas ½.

Warm the jam and spread it over the pudding. Whisk the egg whites until stiff, add half the remaining sugar and whisk again. Fold in nearly all the remaining sugar. Spoon the meringue round the edge of the jam and sprinkle with the remainder of the caster sugar. Return the pudding to the oven for 40–45 minutes or until the meringue is set.

SERVES 4

LEMON MERINGUE PIE

300g /11 oz granulated sugar
45 ml/3 tbsp cornflour
45 ml/3 tbsp plain flour
pinch of salt
300 ml/½ pint water
30 ml/2 tbsp butter
5 ml/1 tsp grated lemon rind
75 ml/3 fl oz lemon juice
3 eggs, separated
75 g/3 oz caster sugar

SHORT CRUST PASTRY
175 g/6 oz plain flour
2.5 ml/½ tsp salt
75 g/3 oz margarine (or half butter, half lard)
flour for rolling out

Set the oven at 200°C/400°F/gas 6. To make the pastry, sift the flour and salt into a bowl, then rub in the margarine until the mixture resembles fine breadcrumbs. Add enough cold water to make a stiff dough. Press the dough together with your fingertips.

Roll out the pastry on a lightly floured surface and use to line a 23 cm/9 inch pie plate. Line the pastry with greaseproof paper and fill with baking beans. Bake 'blind' for 15 minutes, then remove the paper and beans. Return to the oven for 5 minutes.

Meanwhile mix the sugar, cornflour, plain flour and salt in the top of a double boiler. In a saucepan, bring the water to the boil. Stir the boiling water slowly into the dry mixture, then place the top of the double boiler over gently simmering water. Cover and cook gently for 20 minutes.

Draw the pan off the heat and add the butter, lemon rind and juice. Put the egg yolks in a bowl and add a little of the cooked mixture, then add to the mixture in the pan. Beat well, replace over the heat and cook, stirring constantly until thick. Remove the pan from the heat and set aside to cool. Remove the pie from the oven and reduce the oven temperature to 180°C/350°F/gas 4.

In a clean, grease-free bowl, whisk the egg whites until stiff. Fold in the caster sugar. Pour the lemon custard into the baked pastry case and cover the top with the meringue, making sure that it covers the top completely. Bake for 12–15 minutes until the meringue is lightly browned. Leave to cool before cutting.

SERVES 6

TREACLE TART

45 ml/3 tbsp golden syrup
50 g/2 oz soft white breadcrumbs
5 ml/1 tsp lemon juice

SHORTCRUST PASTRY
150 g/5 oz plain flour
2.5 ml/½ tsp salt
65 g/2½ oz margarine (or half butter, half lard)
flour for rolling out

Set the oven at 200°C/400°F/gas 5. To make the pastry, sift the flour and salt into a bowl, then rub in the margarine until the mixture resembles fine breadcrumbs. Add enough cold water to make a stiff dough. Press the dough together with your fingertips.

Roll out the pastry on a lightly floured surface and use just over three quarters of it to line a 20 cm/ 8 inch pie plate, reserving the rest for a lattice topping.

Melt the syrup in a saucepan. Stir in the breadcrumbs and lemon juice, then pour the mixture into the prepared pastry case.

Roll out the reserved pastry to a rectangle and cut into 1 cm/½ inch strips. Arrange in a lattice on top of the tart. Bake for about 30 minutes.

SERVES 6

MRS BEETON'S CHARLOTTE RUSSE

45 ml/3 tbsp icing sugar, sifted
24 sponge fingers
45 ml/3 tbsp water
15 ml/1 tbsp gelatine
500 ml/17 fl oz single cream
45 ml/3 tbsp any sweet liqueur
1 × 15 cm/ 6 inch round sponge cake,
1 cm/½ inch thick

In a small bowl, mix 30 ml/2 tbsp of the icing sugar with a little water to make a thin glacé icing. Cut 4 sponge fingers in half; and dip the rounded ends in the icing. Line a 15 cm/6 inch soufflé dish with the halved fingers, placing them like a star, with the sugared sides uppermost and the iced ends meeting in the centre. Dip one end of each of the remaining biscuits in icing and use to line the sides of the dish, with the sugared sides outward and the iced ends at the base. Trim the biscuits to the height of the dish.

Place the water in a small heatproof bowl and sprinkle the gelatine on to the liquid. Stand the bowl over a saucepan of hot water and stir the gelatine until it has dissolved completely.

Combine the cream, liqueur and remaining icing sugar in a bowl. Add the gelatine and whisk until frothy. Stand the mixture in a cool place until it begins to thicken, then pour carefully into the charlotte. Cover the flavoured cream with the sponge cake round. Place in the refrigerator for 8–12 hours, until firm.

Loosen the biscuits from the sides of the dish with a knife, carefully turn the charlotte out on to a plate and serve.

SERVES 6

ORANGE SOUFFLÉ

2 oranges
75 g/3 oz caster sugar
300 ml/½ pint milk
75 g/3 oz butter
50 g/2 oz plain flour
4 eggs, separated
icing sugar

Set the oven at 190°C/375°F/gas 5.

Finely grate the rind of both oranges. Squeeze the juice of one and put to one side. Add the sugar and grated rind to the milk, heat gently to boiling point, then remove from the heat. Leave to infuse for 5–7 minutes.

Melt the butter in a saucepan, stir in the flour and cook slowly for 2 minutes, without allowing the flour to colour; stir all the time. Add the flavoured milk gradually, stirring constantly, and beat until smooth. Bring the sauce to the boil and add the reserved orange juice. Remove from the heat. Add the yolks to the sauce, one by one, beating well together. Whisk the whites until fairly stiff. Stir 15 ml/ 1 tbsp into the sauce, then fold in the remainder.

Turn the mixture at once into a buttered 1.25 litre/2¼ pint soufflé dish and bake in the oven for about 35–40 minutes until risen and browned. Sprinkle with a little icing sugar, and serve at once.

SERVES 4

SUMMER PUDDING

900 g/2 lb soft red fruit, eg black and red currants, blackberries, raspberries and bilberries
100–175 g/4–6 oz caster sugar
a strip of lemon rind
8–10 slices day-old white bread
(5 mm/¼ inch thick), crusts removed

Put the fruit into a bowl with sugar to taste and the lemon rind, and leave overnight. Turn the fruit and sugar into a pan, discarding the lemon rind, and simmer for 2–3 minutes until very lightly cooked. Remove from the heat.

Cut a circle from one slice of bread to fit the bottom of a 1.5 litre/2¾ pint pudding basin. Line the base and sides of the basin with bread, leaving no spaces. Fill in any gaps with small pieces of bread. Fill with the fruit and any juice it has made while cooking. Cover with bread slices. Place a flat plate and a 900 g/2 lb weight on top, and leave overnight in a refrigerator.

Served turned out, with chilled whipped cream.

SERVES 6–8